sections offer suggestions for further activ...

The projects will throw up many ideas which ...ay not be used in the final pieces, so it is a good idea to save ideas in a resource scrapbook. This might be for the whole class, for groups or individuals. Ideas can be saved in words, notation, recordings and on sequencer, to be referred to in later work. Sections might include 'Offbeat accompaniments in $\frac{2}{4}$, $\frac{3}{4}$, $\frac{4}{4}$, $\frac{7}{8}$', 'New chords', 'New scales', etc.

I would like to thank editor Barry Russell, Lesley Rutherford and all those at Boosey & Hawkes, Dr. Catherine Simpson and David Short for translations and pronunciation guides, Stephen Bull for the Indian ragas, Mark Irwin and Bill Badley for creating the CD, and the other members of *The Carnival Band* – who as always had the best ideas – Giles Lewin, Raphael Mizraki, Andrew 'Jub' Davis and Bill Badley.

Andrew Watts

Area known as the Balkans

CONTENTS

Series Editor **Barry Russell**

BOHEMIA TO THE BALKANS

by Andrew Watts of The Carnival Band

TEACHER'S BOOK

Boosey & Hawkes
Music Publishers Limited
London · New York · Bonn · Sydney · Tokyo

INTRODUCTION

Musicians in both the classical and popular fields have always found inspiration in folk music. It comes as a breath of fresh air, challenging our preconceptions, defying the norms and opening up new possibilities. This collection of projects, based largely on music from the Czech Republic, Slovakia and Macedonia, is intended to give young musicians the chance to encounter a rich diversity of rhythms, scale patterns, harmonies, forms, instrumentation and playing styles. This is merely the tip of the iceberg, however: the possibilities for further exploration of the music of these countries and of Hungary, Poland, Romania, Bulgaria and so on are endless!

Bohemia to the Balkans aims to help pupils acquire new skills of performance, composition, improvisation, arranging, and listening, appraisal and analysis. Basic performances of the original folk tunes lead on to games and exercises of the type that might be done in one of *The Carnival Band*'s workshops. Building on these, pupils create their own arrangements and original compositions. In the process they will analyse the source material and gain an insight into some non-Western, non-classical musical cultures.

In *The Carnival Band* we have taken tunes from Eastern Europe and adapted them to suit our own performance style. Whether these are 'authentic' renditions is immaterial. We play these tunes in our own way because we enjoy them like that, and we hope that users of this pack will likewise feel free to claim ownership of the material.

The CD is an integral part of the publication, intended to simulate some of the elements of our workshops. The purpose of introducing professional musicians into the classroom (whether live or on record) is not to replace the teacher but to be a resource for the class. We hope to share with you whatever precision, flexibility, inventiveness and performance energy we have acquired through our training and our experience on the concert platform and in the recording studio. We are there to encourage pupils to give their performances that extra 'oomph'! To that end we have included some recordings of live performances on the CD.

It is not necessary to work through the projects in sequence as each one is self-contained. Ideas and techniques explored in one project can be used in another: some suggestions are made as to when this is appropriate.

Within each project it is possible to select from the activities suggested rather than attempt them all. Completely satisfactory performances can be made at an early stage and pupils should be encouraged to do this. The material can then be developed as time and ability allow. In this respect, folk music offers great flexibility, with the possibilities ranging from melody alone, to full arrangements requiring considerable instrumental and vocal expertise, and complex compositions based on the original. It is suggested that each project culminates in a series of performances or recordings. Equally, none of the projects exhaust all the possibilities so the *What Next?*

SLOVAK NONSENSE SONG
Skočila mi mníška

This Slovak tune was collected by Bartók, who used it as the basis of *Játék* in his *44 Duos for Two Violins*. The simple melody provides endless scope for creative work in the classroom. We'll move from making simple 'oom-pah' style settings of the melody (using tune, bass and chords) to a more sopisticated exploration of accompaniment. All the material will be based on the original melody, but will eventually make whole new pieces! We're not just making an arrangement of the tune, rather showing young composers how to make the most of their musical ideas.

The words of this song are near-nonsense in meaning, as is common in many of our nursery rhymes, too. It is essentially about a girl who does not wish to be married off to the old widower of her mother's choice, but to the young man God has promised her!

Phonetic translation:
Sko-chi-la mi mneesh-ka, mneeshka do shkor-tsa;
Nʸe-die-ze mnʸa, manka, manka, za doʷ-tsa!
A mnʸe paan boh slu-bu-je,
zhe mnʸe von to da-ru-ye
mlaa-dʸen-tsa.

Learning the tune...

Teach this by ear, in short sections. Splitting the tune up in this way makes it easier to learn and gives a good opportunity to demonstrate how the melody is constructed from a number of small cells. Start by singing to 'la', if you prefer. Once the class can sing the melody ask them to transfer it onto instruments. How many notes does the tune use? Notice the *Three Blind Mice* phrase which acts as a binding feature, a sort of mini chorus, as well as a 'full stop'.

Try exploring different ways of performing the melody, experimenting with:
☆ speed
☆ volume
☆ instrumentation (including sharing the melody between instruments)
☆ articulation
Aim for energy, strong characterisation and tight ensemble!

These first versions could be recorded as performances in their own right. Listen to **track 1** for some performance ideas, but more importantly encourage pupils to make their own decisions.

Explorations and Experiments
Making an accompaniment

Start very simply, using just two notes: G and D. This can be in any
register for now, even though it will ultimately provide material for a bass
line. Work on the first five bars to begin with. Here are some possibilities:

Now try out different rhythms for these bass lines:

Try having groups working separately on the two sections of the tune,
combining them in a full class performance.

'Oom-pah' Chords

Try adding G and D major, following the symbols on the main tune. Guitars
and keyboards can play whole chords while melody instruments share
notes of the triad or move around the triad shape.

At first the chords will probably move with the bass line. When pupils are
confident with their chord progressions, however, make it more lively by
asking the bass line instruments (not necessarily the lowest) to play on the
beat and the others off the beat to produce an 'oom-pah' style of
accompaniment.

Play **the rebound game** to introduce this idea:

☆ set up a regular pulse using a drum, metronome or use **track 2** on
the CD.
☆ playing in time with this, the leader plays a note and the others
'bounce back', keeping in time. (On the CD the double bass is the
leader, the mandolin plays the first few 'bounces' then fades out.)
☆ the leader can wait, or play several notes in succession to try and
catch the others out.

Here's an example:

etc.

This game is great for developing concentration and rhythmic precision. Encourage pupils to use eyes as well as ears to develop their ensemble playing skills. Make the game more or less complex by varying the speed and introducing new rhythm patterns.

The echo game can also be used to generate ideas for the 'oom-pah' accompaniments:

☆ use a footstamp to give the pulse.

☆ the leader then claps different offbeat rhythms which the rest of the group echo.

☆ **track 3** gives some rhythmic ideas to echo (each one is played several times on the drum kit. The bass gives the down beats.)

Working in pairs, pupils can invent other patterns, one playing the downbeat and the other inventing an offbeat idea. See how many different patterns the class can invent and notate them in any suitable way (playing them into a sequencer is a good way to visualise them).

One bar patterns:

Two bar patterns:

Four bar pattern:

Use the ideas from these activities and the bass and chord progressions already developed to make complete 'oom-pah' accompaniments, finally adding the melody. Try to keep the accompaniment light and rhythmical: there's no need to use lots of complicated offbeat patterns. A few simple ideas can sound very effective. Try the effect of the tuned instruments playing one pattern whilst unpitched percussion plays a different one.

Record this performance on tape or in any appropriate notation.

Shadowing

This is another way to accompany the tune. Here, a second line moves in parallel intervals with the melody. Try shadowing in thirds (you can hear this shadowing technique on **track 1** of the CD):

Then get pupils to play the line and its shadow with the accompaniment already invented. Discuss the results: do some of the chords need to be changed? Perhaps the shadow part will need to be altered slightly.

Eastern European folk traditions make use of a wide range of intervals, not just thirds. The class could try shadow parts which start a second, fourth, fifth, sixth and seventh above or below the melody...

Seconds...   Fourths...

Again, ask pupils to try their bass lines with the shadow parts and experiment to find out what works well. This will lead naturally on to the next activity.

New ideas for harmonising the melody can come from these shadowings. For example, a shadowing in fifths will produce:

Chords can be taken from this and used with the existing bass line, or a new bass line can be made to fit them. Pupils can try taking a single chord and bass note as an ostinato figure:

The chord and bass could also be used to imply harmonic shifts:

Here are some examples using accompaniment and tune based on...

Seconds: Fourths:

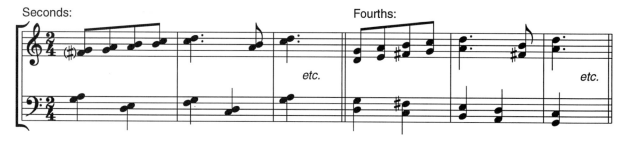

etc.   etc.

Fifths: Sixths:

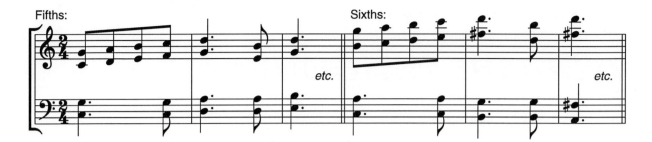

And Sevenths:

Pile up

Two or three adjacent notes from the tune to make new chords:

Or get pupils to pick every other note: this shows the basic structure of melodies (often triadic) and the use of passing notes. Encourage them to be imaginative, look for other shapes hidden in the melody:

Now experiment with these new chords in the class, firstly by moving them stepwise, and by making up a bass and other accompanying patterns to go with them. These could be related to the shape used to make the chord:

It's helpful to keep a scrapbook of these ideas, either on tape, sequencer or in notation, to use as a resource in later work.

Cut and paste

Cutting and pasting will help pupils analyse the melody and make the most of the musical material by deriving further accompaniment ideas from the melody itself. Firstly, pupils can pick short sequences of notes from the tune and try them as accompanying figures...

The fragments can then be transformed in various ways, such as inversion....

and rhythmic augmentation....

Use cut and paste to make whole new versions of the melody. Remind pupils they can repeat ideas, transpose and transform them in other ways:

Or...

Review

By now the class will have a wide range of possibilities on which to draw to make their final versions of *Skočila mi mníška*. Working in groups, they should be able to produce a wide variety of arrangements and original compositions. For example, they could take the various ostinati created in previous activities and use them as the framework of a piece by adding a new melodies to them. When performing the pieces encourage discussion of the music, using questions such as:

"What worked well? Why?"
☆ look at balance, instrumentation, speed, dynamics, length of sections.
☆ encourage the players to be discriminating (it is tempting to include as many different ideas as possible): which ideas work well together to create a satisfying whole?

"Could they improve it? How?"
☆ looking at the answers to the above, consider removing and rearranging sections.
☆ pupils might like to include their own solos.
☆ consider adding percussion if it is not already part of the arrangement.

Rehearse the final versions, make any last adjustments, then perform and record them.

What Next?

Try the ideas from this project with *Chodskà kolečka*, round dances from Chodsko in Bohemia. You can find the music in the appendix, p.36.

CD

✪ **Learn the tune**: by listening to the CD (**track 4**) or from the score. Each section can be learned and worked on separately. Encourage pupils to find shapes which are similar in contour and rhythm and those which are reflections/inversions. Remind them to look out for cut and paste possibilities here.

✪ **Accompaniments** can become more sophisticated: bass lines could use notes from the triad, for example, as well as just the roots of the chords...

(Tune B:)

✪ **Chords** are indicated in the music, but feel free to employ others, such as:

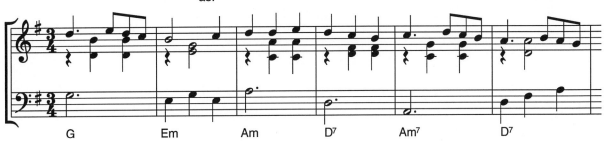

✪ **Offbeat patterns** in triple time will give many new possibilities for accompaniments which can be approached using the same games as previously (p.6-7):

✪ **Shadowing** will work well: pupils can start in thirds, but should also enjoy other possibilities. They can carry on to use chords created by this process in their accompaniments.

✪ **Drones** provide another possibility for making an accompaniment, or pupils could improvise short tunes over a drone. With one or two players holding down a G, others take it in turns to play or sing one or two bar phrases using these notes:

The class could use the echo game and the question and answer game in

which one player plays or sings a short phrase and another answers with
a different phrase:

Try improvising tunes using this set of notes:

Get the class to consider which notes make harmonic clashes with the
drone – they should enjoy these sounds!

Newly composed or improvised melodies over a drone can be
incorporated into the final performances. Combine different ideas and
groups by considering sections which might be heard more than once as
chorus ideas, any changes of tempo, and so on.

THE BELLY DANCER FROM BANJA
Banjski čoček

This project and the next (*Potrčeno*) are based on music from Macedonia, a region which includes the state of Macedonia (formerly part of Yugoslavia) and parts of northern Greece and south western Bulgaria. This area was once part of the Ottoman Empire and its music shows the influence of Turkish culture. The songs and dances of Macedonia use several different scales and many complex rhythms. They can be both hauntingly beautiful and fast and furious. Among the traditional instruments are the **gajde** (bagpipe), **zurle** (a type of oboe), **supeljka** and **kaval** (flutes), **tapan** (large drum) and **tarabuka** (goblet drum). The class could try and find equivalents for these sounds, but the music is suitable for a wide range of instruments and part of the fun of performing it lies in adapting it for whatever instruments are available.

In this project we'll use a wide range of 'new' scale formations, particularly non-Western scales. These open up tremendous possibilities for exploration of melodic and harmonic construction. We'll go on to invent our own scales and make pieces using them.

Between about 1700 and 1900 most Western art music only used two or three scales (major and melodic and harmonic minors). Folk musicians used many more, however.

Pupils may have already explored pentatonic scales in classroom work or encountered chromatic scales if they are learning to play an instrument. A good starting point for work on scales would be to look at the C major scale; (there should be no mystique attached to scales: pupils simply start on middle C, play all the white notes of the keyboard until they reach the next C and – hey presto – a C major scale!). Encourage the class to explore the intervals between notes, but also look at the patterns in the scale (there are two halves, with the second – G, A, B, C – an exact transposition of the first – C, D, E, F).

The scale above is from Macedonia. The open note head shows the usual note for ending a melody using this scale. It is sometimes called the 'final', but 'home note' is a useful term. Point out how the second group of four notes is an exact transposition of the first. Notice, too, the F♮ at the upper end and the F♯ at the lower (shades of the Western harmonic minor scale).

Learn the scale

Start with a few notes at a time, learning by memory. Group chime bars to form the scale, re-arrange notes on idiophones, or use coloured dots on keys and bars – any tricks which help pupils grasp the shape of the scale are fine, but ears are the most important tools! Once the basic scale is known, use the following form which begins and ends with the final (this leads naturally into the melodic patterns found in *Banjski čoček*):

 Banjski čoček practically dances off the page, which helps in learning it by ear! You can hear a performance of it by *The Carnival Band* on **track 5** of the CD. Clap the rhythm patterns before playing fragments which the class can find and echo back. Don't use notation until absolutely essential.

(The slurs are suggestions: they can be changed to suit the instruments available.)

As the class learns the tune make sure they notice the short melodic patterns which are used several times, such as:

These can be learnt separately and used later as ostinati. Encourage the class to remember this point when they make their own melodies – make a little go a long way!

Perform the tune as a single line and discuss with the class how you might colour the melody. For example, keyboards and strings could play bar one, wooden percussion and woodwind bar two, metal percussion and brass bar three and tutti bar four. Try exploring the melody in different octaves, doubled and tripled. Sometimes just single notes or pairs of notes could be doubled.

Accompaniments

An accompaniment can be added simply by playing a G minor / A major chord ostinato throughout. This can be played in a straight four beats or you could use ideas from chapter 1 to create offbeat patterns. Add percussion to build up the ensemble.

Try the music in a variety of styles, setting the ball rolling by playing copying and echoing games (see below) to stimulate rhythmic invention. Experiment with the effect of using rhythms from the melody, perhaps in layers. (We'll come on to more rhythm ideas in Project 3, *Potrčeno.*) One bar units could be used as ostinato patterns, perhaps with inversions or rhythmic augmentations.

Complex patterns can be built up by layering all these ideas: try the effect of layering at the same pitch and at different octaves.

Perform the various versions which have been made. Keep it spontaneous, encouraging different groups to combine their ideas or taking exciting ideas from one group and adding them to another group. Discuss the effects of these instant revisions, and record and/or notate the results as a resource for future work.

Explorations and Experiments
Construction

Here, pupils can build their own melodies using the Macedonian scale. In learning the melody of *Banjski čoček* we discovered that the construction is based on small cells. We can use this idea to build new melodies through improvisation and composition.

Limit the number of notes used in improvisations, starting with two or three before moving on to five or six. Ease of handling is one reason for this limitation but also because resourceful and economical use of material makes for good and effective improvisation. Here are some possible note groups to use in improvisations:

Try to select patterns which fall naturally under the players' fingers. Woodwind players, for example, could use notes which involve the use of only the right or left hand (avoiding the break). Idiophone players need to experiment with convenient stickings. Keyboard players could take two notes in the left hand and three in the right.

First improvisations will lead to the discovery of interesting and satisfying shapes. Encourage economical use of material, in the first instance by repetition. (Echo playing will help this.) **Track 6** gives some short ideas to echo using the following notes:

CD Each idea is played a number of times. Use the following notes to play along with **track 7**:

Continue building melodies using echo and repetition by making your own ideas for pupils to echo as a class, as well as breaking down into smaller groups and eventually into pairs. Here are some initial suggestions for echoing (notice how stepwise movement is used at first and wider intervals later):

Question and answer games also make for satisfying melody construction. Tackle this firstly as 'call and response', with a solo leader calling ideas which the ensemble respond to. Don't worry that this mass reponse doesn't work in combination, it helps to give people confidence (they can hear what they are playing even if you can't). Move on to question and answer playing with individual players. Here's an example:

CD Use **tracks 6** and **7** again, but this time ask pupils to make up new answers to the phrases. Play the game in pairs or a circle with everyone taking a turn. Alternatively, a group or individual could work with the CD, perhaps learning the questions and adding answers to make a call and response melody (echo/repetition could also be used).

Rhythms will initially be free in these improvisations and probably limited to a few possibilities. As improvisations grow into compositions we can explore this element further, again making maximum potential from the material. For example, a short pattern like this:

Can be used in a variety of ways...

(Repetition)　　　　　　　　　　　　　(Mirror image)

(Augmentation)　　　　　　　　　　　　　(Combination)

Processes such as augmentation, diminution, inversion and retrograde can also encourage pupils to make maximum use of material. A melodic idea such as this:

could lead to...

Repetition:　　　　　　　　　　　　　　Inversion: (mirror image)

Transposition:　　　　　Augmenting the shape:　　Decoration:

Combined with the repetition and question and answer ideas, we now have tools to make endless melodies! Experiment with different lengths to find satisfying solutions. Encourage pupils to build contrast of pace and activity into melodies.

Strategies for accompaniment

These are now all in place. We can use the G minor / A major ostinato suggested earlier. This is played on the CD (**track 8**) for pupils to improvise or perform composed melodies over.

CD

These new melodic ideas can also be used as ostinato patterns. Again, experiment with the gamelan-like effect of them all happening in the same octave and then in different octaves. Which effect is preferred?

Vertical combinations of notes from the scale can produce major and minor triads as well as augmented and diminished chords. Experiment also with piling up seconds, fourths, and so on.

Chapter 1 gave ideas for deriving chords from given material (p.9). Try these with pupils' newly invented material. We can also work this process in reverse and make melodic patterns from the new chords they have found:

Build your own scales!

The explorations above will have given pupils a feel for scale formations. They can invent their own by considering patterns of intervals and shapes within a scale. For example, how is this pentatonic scale from Hungary built?

In this mode we see the repeated pattern of semitone / tone:

The natural characteristics of instruments can also lead pupils to the invention of new scales. When the open strings of a violin are transposed into the same octave this gives:

Similarly, the open strings of the guitar produce a pentatonic scale:

Woodwind players can see what scale results when they cover all the holes then lift them one at a time. A descant recorder, for example, produces the following scale which has a rather eastern European flavour:

(The F♯ is flattened due to the 'incorrect' fingering. Make the most of this new tuning – the scales of Macedonia, Albania, Bulgaria and many non-Western cultures are not equal tempered, unlike Western classical scales.)

Brass players could derive scales from the natural harmonics on their instruments ('out of tune' again!).

Ask pupils to experiment with different notes as the 'final' or 'home note' of their scales. This will significantly alter the character of the tunes produced from them.

Now encourage pupils to try making new tunes and accompaniments from these scales.

What next?

✪ The exploration of scales is almost endless! Pupils could continue to improvise and compose using some of the following:

a. Whole tone scales:

b. African tetratonic scales:

c. African pentatonic scales:

d. African hexatonic scales:

e. Medieval church modes:

Dorian   Phrygian   Hypomixolydian

f. Blues scales:

g. Indian ragas:

Malahari   Mayamalara Gowla   Hamsanandhi

✪ Where possible find examples of different scales on record (see *Discography*).

✪ The work on *Banjski čoček* could lead on to a project to discover the influence of Turkish music on the music of South Eastern Europe. Compare the musical styles and forms, and the instruments used.

New rhythms

Before the twentieth century, Western art music tended to ignore much of
the potential of irregular rhythm patterns. But the music of Stravinsky and
Bartók borrowed from folk roots to add to the rhythmic vocabulary of art
music. These 'new' rhythms dance and flow in an irresistible way. After
exploring possible patterns and groupings, we'll go on to use another
Macedonian scale in improvisation and composition in $\frac{7}{8}$ time. Don't forget
to get pupils to move to the music with this project, either by involving
dance or by encouraging movement from the instrumentalists.

Start by performing the following rhythms by tapping on table tops,
slapping on thighs, or if you can, using paired drums such as congas and
bongos, bringing out the accents using a heavier left hand or left hand
plus foot stamp (counting out loud may help). Start with repeated groups
of two and then three quavers before mixing them to form more exciting
rhythms:

$\frac{4}{8}$ **1** 2 **1** 2 | **1** 2 **1** 2 |
    L R **L** R | **L** R **L** R |

$\frac{6}{8}$ **1** 2 3 **1** 2 3 | **1** 2 3 **1** 2 3 |
    L R R **L** R R | **L** R R **L** R R |

$\frac{5}{8}$ **1** 2 3 **1** 2 | **1** 2 3 **1** 2 |
    L R R **L** R | **L** R R **L** R |

$\frac{7}{8}$ **1** 2 3 **1** 2 **1** 2 | **1** 2 3 **1** 2 **1** 2 |
    L R R **L** R **L** R | **L** R R **L** R **L** R |

$\frac{9}{8}$ **1** 2 3 **1** 2 **1** 2 **1** 2 | **1** 2 3 **1** 2 **1** 2 **1** 2 |
    L R R **L** R **L** R **L** R | **L** R R **L** R **L** R **L** R |

Now try these with footstamps on strong beats and hand claps on the
others (this will really help to show the dance character of the patterns).
Try also making new combinations of two and three quaver groups:

$$\frac{2+2+3+2}{8} \quad \text{or} \quad \frac{3+2+3}{8}$$

Learning Potrčeno

CD Play the CD **track 9** to establish the feel of $\frac{7}{8}$. Then, dividing into three
groups, try this rhythm on class drum kit. You can play along with the CD if
this helps initially.

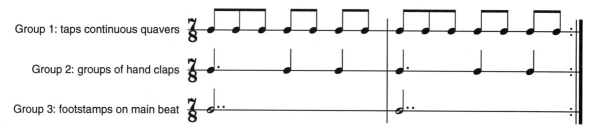

Group 1: taps continuous quavers

Group 2: groups of hand claps

Group 3: footstamps on main beat

When the group is playing (and probably moving) confidently, introduce *Potrčeno*:

You may like to add two or three note slurs to help the music flow and emphasise the dance rhythms.

This exciting dance music from Macedonia is based on the scale:

Using the activities from chapter 2, *Banjski čoček* (p.15-16), explore this scale.

Try the echo and question and answer games using the following segments of the scale:

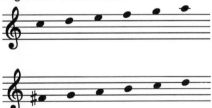

Use **track 10** to show pupils the various melodic fragments that go to make up *Potrčeno*.

Learn in sections: point out that the tune splits into three sections, with each section asking a question twice with different answers each time. (Rehearse the opening leap of a ninth carefully!) Notice that the rhythmic grouping of 3 + 2 + 2 remains constant. Groups could take it in turn to keep the rhythm going while the rest of the class learn the sections in two or three bar chunks. Use body sounds or mix in percussion, perhaps tambourines for the quaver patterns, hand claps for the middle layer and low drums and footstamps for the main beat figure.

Explorations and Experiments

Dividing seven

Dividing a bar into sub groups provides an activity which can help consolidate the learning of notation. Starting with quaver groups, *Potrčeno* is grouped as 3 + 2 + 2 (= 7). Consider how many other combinations are possible... With groupings expressed as equations it is an easy step to convert it into notation:

2 + 2 + 3   becomes

Ask pupils to make a note of the different combinations of seven beats which they discover. The groupings can be shown by accents...

by using longer note values...

or by combinations of single quavers and longer note values...

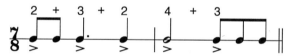

Keep music live! Don't allow this to become just a paper exercise. Have groups swap patterns and perform each other's ⅞ rhythm compositions. Stimulate the composing with echo playing – the whole class or small groups can work at echoing and notating patterns.

Try **track 11** as a backing for more echo work with the class, using some of the patterns below.

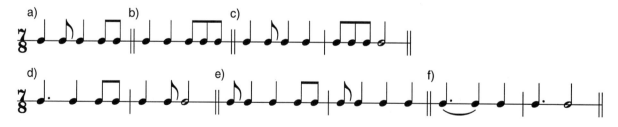

The track can also be used by small groups to make improvisations based on the echoing and question and answer techniques:

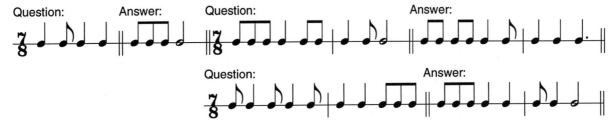

It is a good idea to occasionally remove the safety net of the backing track and see if groups can maintain the pulse themselves.

Concerto grosso... in a circle, the whole group clap and play the 3 + 2 + 2 pattern along with **track 12**. A leader indicates the volume by clapping hands at different heights (head level for loud, waist level for soft). At the sound of the samba whistle on the CD (or any suitable cue if you're not using the CD) one person improvises a break of four bars. The samba whistle then leads the whole group back in with the ostinato rhythm and at the next signal another player improvises a solo. Ask for volunteer soloists to step into the middle of the circle or simply go round the circle one at a time. If you want solos which are longer than four bars, agree that each solo will end with an obvious pattern to lead back into the tutti ostinato, for example:

Layered ostinati can provide richly rhythmic accompaniments for *Potrčeno*. Experiment with busier patterns alongside groupings which use longer note values. Differentiate the lines with contrasting instrumental colours, as here:

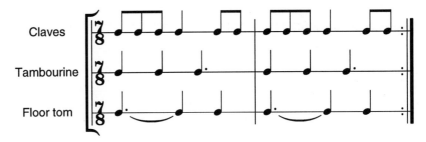

Combine elements from all of the explorations so far to make performances of *Potrčeno* with percussion accompaniment. Percussion solos could be used as an introduction or as solo breaks. Record and/or notate these versions.

Harmony

Pupils can try adding chords of G major and A minor. Sustain the chords for a bar or more and discuss the effect – sometimes one chord can be held for several bars. Enjoy occasional clashes with the melody!

When a chord sequence has been decided, begin to break up the chords, perhaps using the rhythm ideas invented earlier. Play the echo and question and answer games with pitch and rhythm to develop this, using just two or three notes initially (perhaps open strings on violin or guitar). For example:

Here are some more suggestions for echoing and adding answering phrases... Remind pupils that simple patterns make very effective accompaniments!

Ostinato rhythms can be applied to the chord sequence and the patterns layered as before. The original classroom drum kit could be developed as follows, adding pitch:

With the above activities the class will have created a number of short accompanying figures. These could be combined using cut and paste techniques to make longer patterns:

Improvise and compose

To begin improvising solos and composing new melodies using the *Potrčeno* scale, pupils should start by identifying three, four or five note sections of the scale and making patterns with these pitches:

a.

Remind them to look for patterns within the melody itself:

b.

Then, using the group of notes A, try echoing and playing question and answer games with **track 13**. **Track 14** uses the notes from group B.

Track 15 is an ostinato in $\frac{7}{8}$ on a chord of A minor. Ask players to improvise over it, limiting them to just a few notes at first. Keep reminding them that the simplest improvisations are often the most effective!

Pupils can transpose their shapes or improvise new ideas over **track 16**, an ostinato in G major. Try extending this activity further by using both A minor and G major chords, as in the following sequence, on **track 17** of the CD:

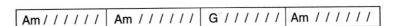

Review

Using these new shapes and the materials they have already created (percussion and chordal accompaniments, melody accompanying figures, ostinati and improvised solo sections), pupils should now be able to make their own arrangements of *Potrčeno*.

☆ Firstly, review all the ideas and begin to assemble the different elements in various ways, perhaps taking parts of one group's work and combining it with another group's.

☆ Suggest starting the piece with a percussion introduction, including improvised sections, or expanding the concerto grosso idea with pitched and unpitched solos, perhaps making the solos into concertino groups.

☆ Encourage pupils to make a plan of the final version (or versions), and decide which instruments will play when. This could be written down as a performing score.

☆ Rehearse the final versions, concentrating particularly on rhythmic accuracy.

☆ After final rehearsals and adjustments, perform and record the works.

What next?

✪ Try looking at other time signatures: $\frac{5}{8}$ is perhaps the most obvious one to choose in connection with Eastern European folk music, but more familiar time signatures can also be used in ways which exploit the groupings already explored in this chapter. For example, a bar of $\frac{9}{8}$ could be divided like this:

✪ Pupils could also experiment with inventing rhythms based on word patterns:

Hun-ga-ry, Po - land, Czech Re-pub - lic

✪ Try adding aspects of the work on scales in the previous chapter to these rhythmic experiments.

✪ Listen to the music of composers such as Stravinsky and Bartók, who were influenced by the rhythms of folk music. Jazz musicans, too, use an increasing complexity of rhythmic structures (as in Dave Brubeck's records *Time Out* and *Time Further Out,* and Don Ellis's *Barnum's Revenge* in $\frac{7}{8}$, *Upstart* and *Indian Lady* in $\frac{5}{4}$). The rhythms of samba and of Indian and African music could also be explored.

BOHEMIAN DANCES
Český tanec

This project calls on skills used in earlier projects and continues to build the pupils' confidence in manipulating sound materials within definite parameters, by looking at variation techniques.

The dances below come from Bohemia in the Czech Republic. Like many folk tunes they can be adapted and arranged to suit whatever instruments are available, and can form the basis of new compositions. On **track 18** of the CD you can hear *The Carnival Band* link these Bohemian dances to a Croatian dance tune called *Drmes* (appendix p.40).

Learning by ear

This is an essential part of this project. Starting with tune A, look for any repeated and transposed ideas. Using keyboards and idiophones, pupils will be able to discover the relationship between the shapes of bar 1 and bar 2; notice also the cadence figure (bar 8) which might seem familiar! Suggest building a simple ostinato accompaniment or drone using the notes G and D, too, if you wish.

Approach tune B in the same way. The shapes here are common to folk melodies the world over, particularly children's rhymes. Consider if any of the melodic shapes have been used elsewhere (...bar 9 is the same as the first phrase of *Polly Put the Kettle On,* bar 12 is the same as the 'my fair lady' refrain from *London Bridge is Falling Down*).

Adding a basic accompaniment at this stage gives a satisfying sense of achievement to a session. Chord symbols are given here but not in the pupil's book: it is a useful exercise to work out which chord fits where, either by ear or by analysing the melodic shapes to find the triadic implications.

Variations

 ***The Carnival Band's* variations**: listen to **track 18** again and discuss any differences between the class performance and *The Carnival Band's* version. Play the track a couple of times and encourage pupils to check the pitch of their version against the recording. Some of the changes were made to suit the instruments available (particularly the violin) and others arose as the musicians enlivened the tunes with their own ideas. Possible answers might include:

- ☆ the pitch is different on the recording
- ☆ ornaments (trills and grace notes) have been added to tune A
- ☆ extra notes have been added to tune A
- ☆ the second section of tune B has been altered

We'll start by looking at these ideas as we make our own variations on *Český tanec*.

Which key is most suitable? Transposition is used firstly to fit material to instruments. Try the tunes starting on different notes to find out which key suits the instruments best. Ease of fingering will be one consideration but encourage the players to also explore different registers and tone colours. For example, compare a shrieking, high clarinet version of the melody with a sombre clarinet in its chalumeau register. If pupils are working in groups, find the key which best suits that combination of instruments and technical capabilities (string players may use open strings for ostinato accompaniments, for example).

On idiophones and keyboards try the effect of moving the melodic shape up or down by step and keeping the same accidentals. This will totally change the character of the melody.

Decorating the melodic line is another simple way of making a variation. Listen to **track 19**, which consists of tune A only. Using the score, identify points in the violin line which have been decorated. Discuss the effect and get pupils to try them on instruments, for example:

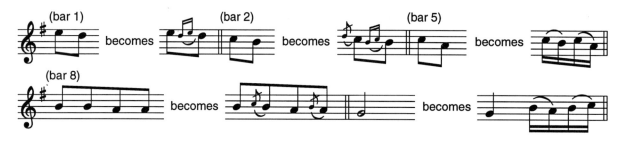

Add ornaments which suit the instrument (not all will work on all instruments) to make decorated versions of the tune. Here's one way of beginning:

Get the class to perform and discuss the ornamented lines, deciding which are the most effective versions. Be careful that they don't add too many ornaments – the line shouldn't seem cluttered!

Tune B is already decorated with semiquaver movement. Try getting pupils to make a simplified version of this tune, using note values of a quaver or longer. The opening might become:

and bars 17 to 18 could be...

Make a note of the material removed from the 'skeleton': this can be used to provide ideas for decorations such as

☆ passing notes (filling in the gaps)...

☆ auxiliary notes (also known as neighbour notes)...

☆ repeated notes...

☆ augmenting stepwise movement with wider leaps:

On **track 20** you can hear tune B with alterations; using the score, ask pupils to find and discuss these. Then, working singly or in groups, pupils can make their own decorated versions of tune B: remind them that folk music is hardly ever played the same way twice!

How fast should the tune go? Variations based on tempo are another simple but effective way of manipulating the material. If you try the effect of playing the tunes at different speeds, you may find that tune A works equally well played quite fast, whereas tune B (or its skeleton) works well as a slow tune with decorations and ornaments.

Altering the instrumentation can totally change the character of the material: perform it on various instruments and different combinations and discuss the timbral qualities. Single types of instrument can work well (try only wooden percussion, for example, or brass alone) and don't be afraid to experiment with new groupings. Move the tune around in the texture – try it in the bass, perhaps, or played in different octaves simultaneously. Remember to vary the accompanying sounds as well.

You could also transfer the tunes to unpitched percussion or percussion which can only reflect the pitch shape to a limited extent, such as three bottles (high, medium and low) for tune A and four large tin cans for tune B. Alternatively, a different sound could be used for each pitch in slow versions of the tune.

How loud should the music be? Dynamic variations can dramatically change the effect of the music. Try a fast variation played loudly and then at whisper level, and compare the intensity of the two. Ask the players to introduce *forte* and *piano* sections into their versions of the tunes – remember the choice and number of instruments will affect the dynamic level, too. Experiment with sudden changes of dynamic level, as well as *crescendi* and *diminuendi* – pupil conductors can control the dynamic changes. Make sure players reduce the volume to a whisper as well as play *fortissimo*!

Review

Pupils will now have explored several ways of varying the tunes and should begin to feel that they are able to manipulate them and make their own pieces. Deciding on an order, perform the dances using some of these variations. Remember, it is not necessary to start with tune A – for example a performance might begin like this:

Slow version tune B	*pp*	glocks with guitar ostinato
Faster version B	*f*	keyboards and percussion
Fast version A	*p*	strings *etc.*

More complex variations

We can now start exploring other aspects of the music's construction to make more complex variations. Up to now, we've kept the basic form of the melodies and made variations in performance, most of which can be made working by ear with a minimum of planning beforehand. The strategies which follow look at more radical ways of varying the material. Here, listening, performance, improvisation and composition all overlap making it important to use playing, writing (notation) and recording to develop pupils' skills. Keep a note of the experiments and findings in a class file or on a display or black/white board as a resource for individual and small group work.

New scales and modes can change the complexion of the melodies in an exciting way. *Český tanec* uses a basic scale of G major (with an occasional C♯ in tune A). Try playing tune A based on the Macedonian scale below, also used in *Banjski čoček* (chapter 2). Here, however, the home note is kept as G, not A.

Tune B can be fitted to the same scale or, as we've done below, to the same scale transposed down a tone. The reason for this transposition is to retain the third note of the scale (G) as the home note, which fits the tune more accurately to the scale.

Tunes fitted rigidly to new scales and modes don't always sound immediately convincing, so suggest changing details to make the new tune 'work'. As an alternative approach we can use the general outline of the melody, either by plotting note heads without a stave but still reflecting the pitches of the tune:
(Tune A bars 1 to 2)

or by drawing lines to represent the shape of the melody...

Play these shapes using scales which were invented or discovered in Project 2, *Banjski čoček*. The shape of tune A used with a pentatonic scale could sound like this:

Tune B could be played using a blues scale, which will completely transform its character. Notice how we've slightly altered the shape:

Change the time signature to alter the metre. To make the tunes fit pupils will have to stretch or compress the rhythms, shorten note values, miss out or repeat notes. They should enjoy the challenge! You could suggest using some of the time signatures and rhythms explored in chapter 3, *Potrčeno,* or use this opportunity to add new ideas to the resource bank (file or display). Here are two examples, the first of which shows stretching, the second compression...

Rhythmic variations can be simply achieved by retaining the pitches of the melody and doubling or halving note values so that, for example,

Slowed down versions of the tunes can be used as accompaniments:

Try 'swinging' straight quavers...

Add dotted rhythms ♩. ♪ (use 'Scotch snap' rhythm as well ♪ ♩.)

Shape variations: use the pitch outlines drawn earlier to work out pitch variations using processes such as augmentation, inversion and reversal. Shapes can also be exaggerated (increasing the distance between notes). Tune A might become:

Alternatively, make the steps between notes smaller:

Inverting the shape of tune B creates a line which fits neatly with the original:

Have fun using the shapes backwards (retrograde) and backwards and upside down (retrograde inversion). As an appropriate adjunct to this work, look at some simple examples of invertable counterpoint in Bach's music or construction of tone rows in Schoenberg, Berg and Webern.

Cut and paste activities, either literal, or on paper or sequencer, encourage creative decision-making in handling musical ideas. In group work, pupils could pool resources and use each other's ideas for this activity. Try a musical game of 'consequences' as an experiment and discuss why this does or doesn't 'work'. As the pupils become more confident in manipulating the musical material they will be able to fragment melodies, select ideas and combine them to form new rhythmic and melodic patterns. Don't forget that units can be repeated, reversed, inverted, augmented and diminished. They should be repositioned to find the best and most satisfying order. Here is an example of a cut and paste melody:

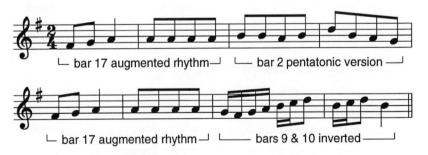

Combine several different variation processes in a single variation. The following examples were derived from a number of procedures.

Tune A was given a new key signature and metre:

A further variation on tune A was created by augmenting the rhythm and fitting it to the $\frac{7}{8}$ time signature:

Sections from the two variations were then cut and pasted to make an entirely new variation which you can hear on the CD as **track 21**.

Varying the accompaniment can make material go further. Encourage players to devise a number of different accompaniments for their variations, trying different speeds and combinations of instruments. Try the same tune slowly with a simple drum ostinato and fast with a full ensemble 'oom-pah' accompaniment. Consider all the ideas which have been created in earlier projects.

Assembling the end product

The group will by now have a wonderful array of options to consider. It is probably a good idea to select a few of the variation processes that seem to be bearing fruit and concentrate on them. The others can be worked on at a later stage or used with one of the tunes in the appendix.

Ask the pupils to assemble their variations into a running order. Individuals or small groups could present a variation each with the whole group playing the main tune as a *ritornello*. You could build up two separate pieces: one based on tune A, the other on tune B, or you could combine the two.

Try and establish an overall structure to the piece. This could be a gradual increase in tempo leading to a furious finale, for example. Another possibility would be to build on contrasts of loud and soft variations. Or perhaps the variations could begin with those closest to the original tunes (i.e. decorated versions of the melody) moving on to the more distantly related variations, before returning to the original.

Remind pupils to characterise their variations with different instrumental colours, dynamics and tempi. Scores could be made using conventional notation or other suitable symbols.

As the piece or pieces are rehearsed, further refinements will be made. When everything is going well, perform the new works and record them.

What next?

The ideas explored in this project (and those from earlier chapters) can also be used in conjunction with the selection of Eastern European tunes in the appendix, or are equally appropriate for use with material from a variety of cultures. They can, of course, be used with pupils' original compositions, too.

APPENDIX

ROUND DANCES FROM CHODSKO Chodskà kolečka

These tunes from Chodsko in the Czech Republic can be played
separately or combined to make a longer structure. You can hear *The
Carnival Band* perform them on **track 4** of the CD. See 'What Next?' in
chapter 1 (p.11) for ideas on creating an accompaniment and improvising
over drones.

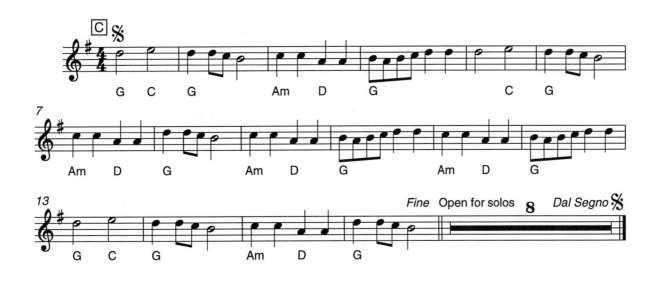

THE OLD WOMAN'S CHRISTENING
(Staro žensko krsteno)

This Macedonian tune can be heard on **track 22** of the CD. It is based on two scales, with the change between them coming at bar 55. It is a long piece so experiment with altering the instrumentation as well as building up the speed. Pupils could improvise or compose their own four bar sections to add into the piece or make up their own final section using the second scale.

Nb. The unusual key signature!

On track 22 of the CD, *The Carnival Band* perform this piece with an ostinato bassline, from which the chord symbols here are taken. Likewise, the chords are often played as a bare fifth, so the major/minor tonality is implied only by the melody line. The chord symbols are, therefore, just a suggestion which fits this particular performance.

SHAKING DANCE (Drmes)

This dance tune from Croatia can stand on its own or be combined with the Bohemian dances (chapter 4) as on **track 18** of the CD. The tune is made up of short melodic fragments which can be manipulated and transformed to make new compositions (see chapter 4 for further ideas). The accompaniment can be kept very simple but should be played with rhythmic vitality to drive the piece along (see chapter 1 for ideas on simple accompaniments).

RINGS AROUND THE MOON (Okolo měsíce)

Another chance to try some vocals! This piece (**track 23** of the CD) is
something of a curiosity as it comes from Czech settlers in Texas! It's not
known whether this tune was taken from Eastern Europe or if was derived
in Texas, but the meaning of the words is approximate due to the
corruption to the original language. Pupils could try adding offbeat
accompaniments (as explored in chapter 1), making up English words for
the middle section, or perhaps composing their own middle sections to
extend the piece (making a A B A C A D A structure).

Translation:
Around the moon circles are forming
those girls of ours, those girls of ours
cannot be consoled
those girls of ours, those girls of ours
are looking for thousands.

Phonetic translation:
Okolo mnʸe-see-tse ko-la se dʸe-la-yee
ti na-she pa-nen-ki, ty na-she pa-nen-ki
tee-shit se ne-da-yee
ti na-she pa-nen-ki, ty na-she pa-nen-ki
ti-see-tse hle-da-yee.

DISCOGRAPHY

Many large record shops now have a section, usually labelled *World Music*, in which recordings of folk music and folk-inspired music from non-Western countries can be found. This is a very short selection from a long list of titles currently available in the UK. You could try asking friends who take their holidays in Eastern Europe to look out for interesting records which may not be available here!

Field recordings and historic recordings

Some of these uncompromising tracks are not easy listening, but there is nothing like hearing the real thing to stimulate fresh ideas.

Various artists: *Romania – Music for Strings from Trannsylvania*
Le Chant du Monde LDX 274937

Various artists: *Ukrainian Village Music* *(Historic Recordings 1928-1933)*
Arhoolie Folklyric CD7030

Various artists: *Bosnia – Echoes from an Endangered World*
Smithsonian Folkways SF40407

Studio recordings by contemporary artists from Eastern and South Eastern Europe

Marta Sebestyen: *Muzsikas*   Hannibal Records HNCD 1330

Various artists: *Balkana, The Music of Bulgaria*   Hannibal Records HNCD 1363

Méta and Kálmán Balogh: *Gypsy Music from Hungarian Villages*   Arc Music EUCD 1073

The Dmitri Pokrovsky Ensemble (Russia): *The Wild Field*   Real World Records CDRW17

Artists blending folk music with jazz and rock influences

Kalesijski Svuci: *Bosnia Breakdown*   Ace Records/Globestyle CDORBD074

Ivo Papasov and His Orchestra: *Balkanology*   Hannibal Records HNCD1363

British based ensembles influenced by the music of the Balkans

Orbestra: *Transdanubian Swineherds*   Hannibal Records HNCD1367

Three Mustaphas Three: *Soup of the Century*   Fez-o-phone Records CDFEZ004

BIBLIOGRAPHY

To find out more about Bartók, the folk song collector, try:
Bartok: His Life and Times by Hamish Milne, Omnibus (ISBN 0711902607)

For a flavour of the countries visited in this book try the AA (Automobile Association) **Essential Guides to Hungary, Bulgaria** and **the Czech Republic.**

For a real taste of these countries:
Food and Cookery in Eastern Europe by Lesley Chamberlain, Penguin Books (ISBN 0140468137)

If the chapter on rhythm has whetted appetites for more spicy rhythms:
Learn to Play the Latin American Way by Ronald Hanmer, Studio Music (ISBN 0905925009).

There's more about folk percussion instruments in:
Percussion Instruments and their History by James Blades, Kahn and Averil (ISBN 0871082366)

...for wind instruments:
Woodwind Instruments and their History by Anthony Baines, Dover Publications (ISBN 0486268853)

...and for brass instruments:
Brass Instruments, their History and Development by Anthony Baines, Dover (ISBN 0486275744)

For a guide to typical dance steps:
European Folk Dance by Nigel S. Jaffe, Folk Dance Enterprises (ISBN 0946247153)

Illustrations **Helen Chown**

Cover design **Mike Feeney**

Music setting **Halstan   & Co. Ltd.**